WHAT

NOT

TO

SAY

A Compendium of the
Worst Possible Things
You Can Utter Aloud

KNOCK
KNOCK.
VENICE, CALIFORNIA

CONTENTS

CONTENTS

CONTENTS

INTRODUCTION

**"Writing introductions is a huge waste of time—
no one ever reads them anyway."**

This sentiment, however true, is a perfect example of
what *not* to say to someone writing an introduction to a
book. This statement will *not* be gratefully received by the
person who actually has to write the introduction. It will
not be seen as an example of one's wisdom and sagacity,
or even well-intentioned helpfulness. In fact, if someone
utters these words, it will merely irritate, annoy, offend,
and possibly even anger the poor introduction-writer.

Given the fact that most of us would prefer not to
irritate, annoy, offend, or anger people in our day-to-day
encounters, this book provides some useful advice—a
compendium of phrases that you should never utter.

Unless you've taken a vow of silence at an ashram or
are pleading the fifth in a courtroom, you're probably
susceptible to putting your proverbial foot in your
proverbial mouth. We've all had moments in which we've
uttered thoughtless, ignorant, insensitive, tactless, entitled,
or just plain bone-headed remarks.

That's where this book comes to the rescue. It's a handy
reference guide for what to avoid saying in situations

ranging from dinner parties to cultural events to back-to-school nights; a cheat sheet of no-go remarks when talking to people from a cop to a coworker to a cat lady.

For instance, on a first date, "You look just like my ex" is a nonstarter. It's also probably best to rule out anything like "She's an animal in bed" when talking to your in-laws. And never ask a hipster "How long have you been a hipster?" You might get punched in the face with a growler full of microbrew.

Verbal gaffes are just one component of this book. In addition to a list of specific phrases that you should eschew, there are helpful sidebars with tips, tricks, and cautionary tales. And featured throughout the book are ten things one should never, ever, verbalize under any circumstances—a veritable Hall of Fame of what not to say.

As turn-of-the-century horticulturalist and noted conversationalist Lady Dorothy Nevill remarked, "The real art of conversation is not only to say the right thing at the right place but to leave unsaid the wrong thing at the tempting moment." Or, take to heart this quote attributed to Abraham Lincoln: "Better to remain silent and be thought a fool than to speak out and remove all doubt."

WHAT NOT TO SAY
TO ANYBODY, EVER

I'm telling you this for your own good.

ANGRY PERSON

1. Calm down!

2. I'm rubber, you're glue…

3. Guess those anger management classes didn't work.

4. You and what army?

5. Love those neck tendons!

6. Let's turn that frown upside down!

7. Did the steroids shrink your testicles?

8. You're so cute when you're mad!

9. Wanna take this outside?

10. I know you are, but what am I?

1 Oh, I've heard about your kid.

2 Frankly, my child just isn't challenged
   by ordinary classwork.

3 When do we get to drink?

4 We're planning to homeschool next year.

5 The teachers are a lot younger and
   hotter than when I was in school.

6 That's quite a shriek your kid has.

7 He's your grandson, right?

8 Your kid sure is big for her age.

9 Tell me the truth—do I look high to you?

10 This was our fallback.

SMART GUYS
FINISH LAST

Even the brains at MIT's Media Lab can learn something new, like what not to say on your brand swag. At a 2013 SXSW conference party, guests were given wristbands with phrases like "That's a nice dress. It would look great on my floor" and "Do you wash your clothes with Windex? 'Cause I can see myself in your pants." It was the venue's idea, not something the MIT staff had hatched, but it led to Twitter outrage and a quick apology. Stating that "the Media Lab is firmly committed to supporting women in the sciences, computing, arts, and engineering. We don't like—and certainly don't want to support or disseminate—offensive messaging," MIT, with their public mea culpa, showed a good way to defuse a situation in which they'd promoted a sexist mindset.

WHAT NOT TO SAY AT A

BAR

1. Can I give you a tour of the bathroom?

2. Let me show you how to *really* hit on someone.

3. Fight!

4. Golly, I get drunk so easily.

5. Why don't you want to see *my* ID?

6. Can you change the channel to CSPAN?

7. I'll need a few more drinks before I can hit on you.

8. You're drunk already?

9. Can I give you my number? Please?

10. I think I'm going to throw up.

WHAT NOT TO SAY AT THE

BEACH

1. It's great that they make bikinis in your size now.

2. Don't you hate getting sand in your crotch?

3. You're going to need SPF 100.

4. Can I help you apply sunscreen?

5. You should get that thing looked at.

6. Can I get you a cover-up?

7. I know a great bikini waxer if you need a recommendation.

8. You're so brave to wear that suit!

9. No one minds if you pee in the water.

10. Shark!

1 That's not my job.

2 You think you need an assistant? *I* need an assistant!

3 Oh, I had it in my calendar for *next* week.

4 I was out so late last night, I had to sleep in!

5 It wasn't my fault!

6 That's above my pay grade.

7 I thought we canceled that project.

8 I forgot to back it up.

9 I really need a personal day.

10 Good, fast, cheap: pick two.

AVOID THE HALF-COMPLIMENT

People wishing to give the impression that in the search for a soul mate "looks don't matter" might end up going a little overboard while trying to keep it real. According to *Glamour* magazine, going out of your way to avoid sounding as though you're flattering a potential partner is just as bad, if not worse, than openly insulting her. For instance, telling a possible conquest "I'm not looking for a supermodel" or "I don't care that much about beauty" might be intended to make you sound down-to-earth. Instead, all it does is tell her that she's average. Save those kinds of qualifiers for a used-car lot, not the dating pool.

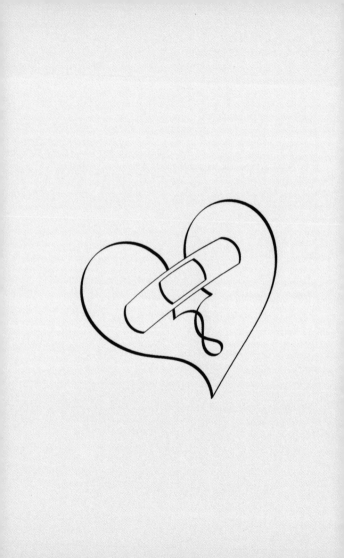

WHAT NOT TO SAY DURING A

BREAKUP

1 It's not you, it's me.

2 You're more in love with me than I am with you.

3 My mother says I deserve better.

4 You're just not "the one."

5 I think I might be gay.

6 I think I might be straight.

7 I used to think your idiosyncrasies were cute—
  now they just bug me.

8 I'll just end up hurting you.

9 I don't want to ruin you for other people.

10 There's someone else.

WHAT NOT TO SAY
TO ANYBODY, EVER

Snap out of it!

WHAT NOT TO SAY TO YOUR

CAT

1. Here, kitty, kitty.

2. Come.

3. Sit.

4. Roll over.

5. Stay.

6. Speak!

7. Go outside.

8. Walkies!

9. Cuddle with me.

10. Do you love me?

WHAT NOT TO SAY TO A

CAT LADY

1. I hate cats.

2. You know what they say about cat ladies.

3. You might as well announce that you never plan to get married.

4. How many are you planning to have?

5. Ugh. Hairballs are so gross.

6. I'm "allergic to cats."

7. Dogs are so much *friendlier*!

8. What are you going to do with them when you have kids?

9. I can tell you have cats.

10. How do you stand the smell?

IT'S BAD LUCK TO SAY GOOD LUCK

There's a rich history of superstition in the theatre about things one should never say. In fact, artists around the world consider "good luck" to be akin to a curse. Instead, for actors, "break a leg" is the appropriate pre-curtain sentiment, while dancers appreciate a hearty *merde* (French for excrement). Opera singers should be wished *toi toi toi* (an onomatopoetic phrase imitating the sound of spitting). And on a side note, a time-honored theatre tradition espouses that uttering aloud the name of the Shakespeare play *Macbeth* is as bad as a breaking a mirror under a ladder while holding a black cat. Instead, refer to it as "The Scottish Play."

WHAT NOT TO SAY TO YOUR
CHILD

1. I miss being your age and not knowing things.

2. If you're going to say bad words, be sure to use them correctly.

3. We did more fun things before you were born.

4. Sorry, the Tooth Fairy had a lot of pillows to visit last night.

5. I named all of my gray hairs after you.

6. Childless adults get to sleep in.

7. You think school is hard? Wait until real life.

8. Science has never disproved the existence of the monster under your bed.

9. You get to drink this many cocktails after you have kids.

10. How many cookies will it take for you to go away?

WHAT NOT TO SAY IN

CHURCH

1 I'm starving. When do we get those crackers?

2 I thought it was a suggestion box they were passing around.

3 I'm not wearing any underwear.

4 Are these good priests or bad priests?

5 Do you really believe in all this stuff?

6 I think the mushrooms are starting to kick in.

7 You call that wine?

8 Hail, Satan!

9 I wish I could only work one day a week.

10 Is this gonna take long?

SOME PEOPLE LIKE IT OPEN-FACED

Sometimes professional situations require honesty above kindness. If you absolutely *must* say something not so nice, try a buffering technique known as the praise sandwich—sandwiching criticism between two layers of praise. It's a popular technique thought to soften the sting of negative feedback. However, some people are on the critical equivalent of a low-carb diet. These jaded targets may prefer you get right to the hearty filling because they use the criticism to spur themselves to new levels of mastery. But more sensitive souls still want a buffer before and after, so try to judge someone's appetite for straight talk before you offer up any disapproval.

WHAT NOT TO SAY AT A

COFFEE SHOP

1. I'll be paying in pennies.

2. I'm sure you'll find a job eventually.

3. My uncle had a heart attack because he drank too much coffee.

4. Cow's milk? Really?

5. I'll have a fat-free iced caramel macchiato, upside down.

6. They don't really care if you sit here all day.

7. The coffee next door's a lot better; I'm only here for the wireless.

8. At these prices, I could buy my own espresso machine.

9. It's not like you do anything to earn tips.

10. Why do I need to buy something?

WHAT NOT TO SAY TO A

COP

1. Do you know who I am?

2. It *should* be legal.

3. It was an honest mistake.

4. You realize I pay your salary, right?

5. It's for my glaucoma.

6. I was just going with the flow of traffic.

7. I guess it depends on what your definition of "stop" is, Officer.

8. That's not booze—my kombucha just smells like that!

9. That pedestrian came out of nowhere!

10. Don't tase me, bro!

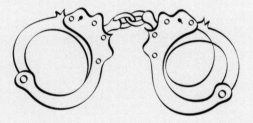

WHAT NOT TO SAY
TO ANYBODY, EVER

Don't
take this
personally.

WHAT NOT TO SAY IN A
COURTROOM

1. I've got a bad feeling about this.

2. Sorry, I have to take this call.

3. Do I have to swear if I'm not religious?

4. Where's Judge Judy?

5. Take my word for it.

6. I could really use a drink.

7. If O. J. can get off, you'll be fine.

8. I think I know that juror.

9. I hate cops.

10. Does Domino's deliver to this courtroom?

WHAT NOT TO SAY TO A
COWORKER

<u>1</u> Your concept of "work attire" is very interesting.

<u>2</u> You know, I'm really not feeling so well.

<u>3</u> Well, if you're fired, at least you can get unemployment.

<u>4</u> This isn't personal—it's business.

<u>5</u> You really put the "ass" in "assistant"!

<u>6</u> This is so impressive…for you.

<u>7</u> How much are you getting paid?

<u>8</u> This is just my day job.

<u>9</u> You might want to wait a while before you use the bathroom.

<u>10</u> I think flu shots *make* you sick.

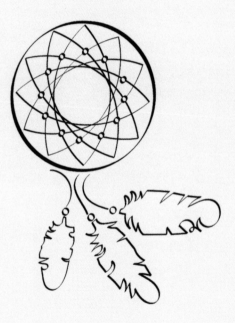

1 I used to make those all the time.

2 This looks pretty flimsy.

3 I saw this somewhere else for much less.

4 Are you on Etsy?

5 This smells weird.

6 Where do you get your supplies?

7 Will you teach me how to do that?

8 That's so easy to do.

9 How's your little "art" business going?

10 Are the ingredients all organic?

1. The book was better.

2. This reminds me of my time in prison.

3. Is this one of those nude performances?

4. I had a dream just like this when I got food poisoning.

5. Wait, this is nothing like wrestling.

6. So, these are the people who couldn't play sports.

7. I just ate a whole can of beans.

8. If I start snoring, just nudge me.

9. I guess theater really is dying.

10. I'm going to Instagram this.

It *should* go without saying that one can't assume that phone calls, emails, or texts are private. However, some people never learn. The result can be highly embarrassing, even career-ending. In 2015 powerful studio executive Amy Pascal was forced to step down as head of Sony Pictures when her private emails were hacked and released, revealing racist, sexist, and just plain old mean comments about President Obama, Jennifer Lawrence, and Angelina Jolie. And, of course, in 2011 married Congressman Anthony Weiner became an ongoing punch line over his repeated sexting of dirty pics to a woman not his wife. Clearly, he didn't wise up, repeating his error a few years later, effectively ending his career over what the press gleefully termed "Weinergate."

PRIVATE AFFAIRS

Sometimes, it doesn't matter what you say, only when and where you say it. One unfortunate hotel worker was fired from his job when he mentioned to a friend how a prominent guest, the actress Jennifer Aniston, was "very sweet and much more petite than I had thought." But this ostensible compliment violated the hotel's strict privacy policy. Because the hotel highly valued its discretion, even a positive comment was tacit acknowledgment that she had been there at all. Proof that knowing when to speak—and when to be discreet—is a key component in knowing what not to say.

WHAT NOT TO SAY DURING A

DINNER PARTY

1. Whoever guesses the secret ingredient can take home the pelt.

2. Uh-oh. I hope no one ate the shrimp.

3. I like to pray before every meal…to Satan.

4. Let's talk politics!

5. Our dog likes to sit at the head of the table.

6. I brought a nice bottle of red…Mountain Dew.

7. I had takeout earlier.

8. Would you mind cooking this steak a little more?

9. Oh, this *is* the main course.

10. Before I start eating—your toilet works fine, doesn't it?

WHAT NOT TO SAY TO YOUR

DOCTOR

1 I know what I have—I looked it up on the internet.

2 My brother-in-law had the same thing
and here's what his doctor said.

3 How much drinking do you consider "social"?

4 I just need another opinion—the other doctors
are all wrong.

5 There's this new pill I saw advertised on TV…

6 I only use it recreationally.

7 There's definitely something wrong with your scale.

8 I'd like to work out, but there's just no time.

9 I accidentally dropped all my painkillers in the toilet.

10 My medications? Well, there's a little white one,
and…

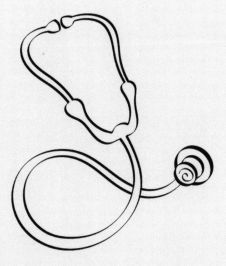

WHAT NOT TO SAY
TO ANYBODY, EVER

You'd better
sit down.

1 I don't want to break her wild, creative spirit.

2 I insist on keeping my dog's manhood intact.

3 Most dogs are fine—it's the *owners* who need training.

4 My dog is a vegan like me, naturally.

5 I tried to teach him, but he has a mind of his own!

6 Those ten are mine.

7 He's a great li'l humper, isn't he?!

8 My dog is actually really, really smart. No, really.

9 Purebred dogs usually have medical issues—
   a rescue is much better.

10 I'm not picking that up.

WHAT NOT TO SAY AT A
FAMILY GATHERING

1. I figured I'd see all of you here or at the next funeral.

2. Are we eating the same thing as last time?
   Because that gave me the squirts.

3. Is it a problem if I move back in?

4. What hashtag should I use to tweet about this?

5. Made any changes to your will?

6. Is this going to go on much longer?

7. You've come a long way since those diary entries I read.

8. My therapist was right.

9. So, anyone transitioning?

10. Being here means I get to skip Thanksgiving, right?

1. You look just like my ex.

2. Does this look infected to you?

3. My parents said I could stay out past ten.

4. Is it okay if I bring my kid?

5. You're paying, right?

6. It's nice to finally be around other human beings again.

7. Did you fart?

8. That wasn't a recent photo of you at all.

9. I figured we could hit the strip club after this.

10. So how many people have you slept with?

DON'T BE RUDE, DUDE

Not only do the phrases in this book get you into trouble if actually spoken, their reach in the workplace may extend beyond the momentary sting. A University of Florida study found that being rudely spoken to negatively impacted problem-solving and creativity skills, even when the rudeness was merely imagined. And it follows that diminished productivity directly affects workflow. According to a Georgetown University study, it was shown that workers will avoid coworkers—or even work—just to dodge more rudeness. The bottom line? The bottom line is positively affected when negativity is banished.

WHAT NOT TO SAY TO A

FOOD SNOB

1 You're a foodie!

2 The secret ingredient is canned cream of mushroom soup.

3 No, it's not organic.

4 I don't like a bunch of weird spices and flavors.

5 Shredded cheese in the can is just so much easier!

6 Two words: slow cooker.

7 I prefer iceberg lettuce.

8 Ewwwww! That looks disgusting.

9 Cilantro tastes like soap.

10 Do you seriously like kale?

1 You just need to lose a little weight.

2 I just assumed you couldn't go.

3 But you two always seemed so happy!

4 You busy next weekend? I'm moving.

5 Oh, this is a couples-only thing, sorry.

6 So how much did you pay for that?

7 He is definitely not good enough for you.

8 You're so good looking! I can't believe you aren't married yet.

9 Since when do you two get together without *me?*

10 I never thought that job was right for you.

NERD IS THE WORD

Much parsing of the terms *nerd*, *geek*, *dweeb*, and *dork* have been hashed out (on the internet, of course), but this seems to be the consensus: Turns out nerds and geeks aren't so uncool anymore. They have sort of a reverse cachet now (or at least they'd like to think so). A nerd is an out-of-the-mainstream iconoclast with intellectual and eclectic interests. A geek is a nerd who specializes in an area of extreme passion or interest. Dweebs and dorks, however, have none of the new cachet of nerds and geeks—they are losers; unlike nerds and geeks, they *want* to be in the mainstream but have no social skills that would enable them to do so. Now you know which terms to avoid.

WHAT NOT TO SAY AT A

FUNERAL

1. [Humming "Ding Dong the Witch Is Dead"]

2. How long before I can hit on the widow?

3. Is there a bar here?

4. Well, if this doesn't convince me to give up smoking, nothing will.

5. I'm surprised he lived this long.

6. So that's what she looks like with clothes on.

7. It's a shame he's in Hell.

8. Do you think anyone has nabbed her apartment yet?

9. They better have a decent spread after this.

10. YOLO!

WHAT NOT TO SAY
TO ANYBODY, EVER

I don't
want to
criticize…

WHAT NOT TO SAY AT THE

GYM

1. May I watch?

2. I looked pretty awkward the first time I used that machine too.

3. Did you wash those shorts after your last workout?

4. THAT'S MY TREADMILL!

5. I think this class is too hard for you.

6. Are you supposed to be making that noise?

7. Let me give you some tips on your form.

8. If you want to lose weight, you're going to have to diet too.

9. The StairMaster is doing great things for your butt.

10. You need a better sports bra.

1. How long have you been a hipster?

2. We're all out of microbrews.

3. You *have* showered, right?

4. I love your man purse.

5. I'm really into the new Justin Bieber album.

6. I don't recycle.

7. Can I friend you on MySpace?

8. That man bun looks great on you.

9. Can I borrow your growler?

10. Did you get that at Target?

1 Do you mind if I film this?

2 Can I smoke in here?

3 You shouldn't trust Western medicine.

4 Can I watch you get a sponge bath?

5 Don't get addicted to painkillers.

6 That scar will make a great conversation starter.

7 Got any bedsores yet?

8 I think that's infected.

9 Are your bowel movements okay?

10 That's what happens when you don't get vaccinated.

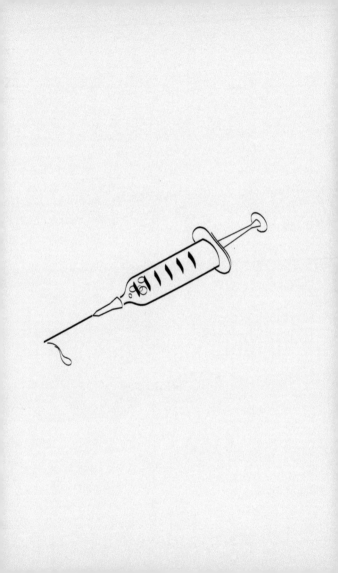

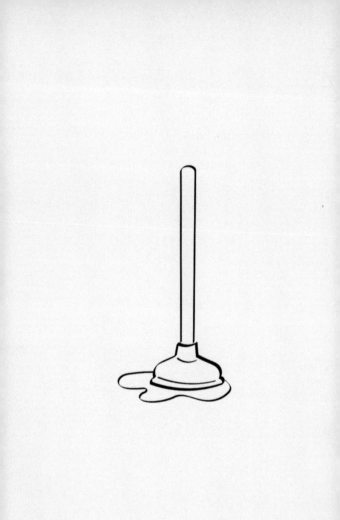

WHAT NOT TO SAY WHEN YOU'RE A

HOUSEGUEST

1. It's only a little blood.

2. You're going to need a new plunger.

3. I'm flattered that you didn't feel the need to clean for me.

4. Can I help you clean your house?

5. Weren't expecting guests, were you?

6. The liquor cabinet is locked.

7. At least you're cheaper than a hotel.

8. Do you have any good porn?

9. Can I recommend an interior decorator?

10. Do you feel the evil spirits in here, too?

BRINGING IT HOME

Regional insults have been around since one
Neanderthal said that the other Neanderthals
who live over the hill smell funny. Regional
insults can go from the macro: "Canada is a
country so square that even the female imper-
sonators are women" (Richard Brenner); to
the micro: "I once spent a year in Philadelphia,
I think it was on a Sunday" (W. C. Fields). You
may think that if the joke is really funny, or
really universal, it's okay to insult someone's
background or hometown. But keep in mind
people's loyalties run deep. Whether it's a home
city, state, region, or country jibe, avoid the all-too-
personal reference (even if it *is* really funny).

HUSBAND

<u>1</u> Is *that* what you're wearing?

<u>2</u> You would if you really loved me.

<u>3</u> Aren't you a little old for that?

<u>4</u> I've trained you well.

<u>5</u> My mother warned me about you.

<u>6</u> If I've told you once, I've told you a thousand times…

<u>7</u> Where do *you* wanna go for dinner?

<u>8</u> Which of my friends do you think is the hottest?

<u>9</u> You want me to do *what* to you?

<u>10</u> Does this make me look fat?

1 I love him more than you do.

2 Do you know why she's so frigid?

3 We think polyamory is an intriguing idea.

4 Is that the guy she lost her virginity to?

5 Can you believe he was still a virgin when we met?

6 My first in-laws were a lot richer.

7 It's almost as good as my mom's food.

8 Do you have decent long-term-care insurance?

9 So, how much is in the will?

10 She's an animal in bed.

It's not just awkward if you accidentally insult the appearance of an employee—you could be sued for sex discrimination. Though state supreme courts have long upheld that employers have some legal leeway when creating "appearance" policies, using "community standards" of attractiveness, another court has held that discrimination based on looks can be actionable. As part of the 2005 decision in *Yanowitz vs. L'Oreal,* the California Supreme Court held that "an explicit order to fire a female employee for failing to meet a male executive's personal standards for sexual desirability is sex discrimination."

WHAT NOT TO SAY
TO ANYBODY, EVER

Is it in?

<u>1</u> Is this gruel organic?

<u>2</u> I really like you…but just as a friend.

<u>3</u> How many cigarettes for a pickaxe, Warden?

<u>4</u> This toilet wine tastes like shit.

<u>5</u> Oh, there must be a mistake…I asked for a single.

<u>6</u> So who do I have to kill around here to pull library duty?

<u>7</u> Can I get that shiv back at the end of the day?

<u>8</u> The guards are very nice here if you just make an effort.

<u>9</u> I think I'll join a gang today.

<u>10</u> "Time off for good behavior?" Then I'm going to be the best prisoner ever!

WHAT NOT TO SAY AT A

JOB INTERVIEW

1 Do you do random drug testing?

2 I know I'm really good looking, but I'm smart, too.

3 My psychic said I should apply for this job.

4 Didn't I go out with your daughter?

5 What's your policy on employees hooking up?

6 My old coworkers were all idiots.

7 That's a dumb question.

8 Nobody really needs a college degree.

9 How strict is your sexual harassment policy?

10 Are you kidding about this salary?

1 You look great for your age.

2 Your hands are so small!

3 Getting a little thin on top, aren't you?

4 You have such a nice face.

5 You aren't defined by your job.

6 It must be hard to stay home while your wife works.

7 It's just a game.

8 I'm so much taller than you!

9 You're such a mama's boy.

10 Men!

DEATH BE NOT PROUD

Other cultures can often teach us ways to say what needs to be said without actually saying it in so many words. According to British actor and writer Stephen Fry, many UK newspaper obituaries, in order to not embarrass the memory of the recently deceased, once used code words to describe their subjects' most distasteful qualities. For instance, if you read between the lines you'd know "a tireless raconteur" is code for "a crashing bore"; that describing someone as "convivial" meant they were a drunk; and one who "gave colorful accounts of his exploits" was, in fact, a known liar.

1. I don't get it.

2. Is it upside down?

3. Can I touch it?

4. My kid could have painted this.

5. We didn't pay to get in here, did we?

6. Where's the gift shop?

7. You call that art?

8. Is this that Banksy guy?

9. That's so po-mo.

10. I think I see boobs.

WHAT NOT TO SAY TO A

NEIGHBOR

1 You know what they say about "good fences."

2 We love the light—and hate window coverings.

3 Hope you like fresh eggs—we're getting chickens!

4 We prefer a clothing-optional lifestyle.

5 Want to see my underground bunker?

6 We'll move those cars out of the front yard
   as soon as they're fixed.

7 You know, I can see right into your bedroom.

8 Great news! My kid is starting a band!

9 Great news! We're starting a day care center!

10 Great news! We're starting a doggy day care center!

WHAT NOT TO SAY TO A

NEW PARENT

1. My kid went through an ugly phase, too.

2. Did you adopt?

3. Is it a boy or a girl?

4. I know what you mean; I have a dog.

5. Are you ready to have another?

6. It's okay, I'm not contagious anymore.

7. Did it hurt?

8. Who's the father?

9. When do you think you'll have sex again?

10. I never want kids.

Despite the 1993 *New Yorker* cartoon proclaiming "On the internet, nobody knows you're a dog," truly anonymous online commenting is a thing of the past. In a 2012 Texas lawsuit, a day spa owner married to a prominent attorney sued anonymous commenters over posts claiming the couple were sexual deviants, molesters, and drug dealers. The haters were unmasked and initially slammed with almost $14 million in damages. The lesson remains: you can hide your name, but not your IP address.

WHAT NOT TO SAY
TO ANYBODY, EVER

It's all in
your head.

WHAT NOT TO SAY AT AN

NRA CONVENTION

1. Can you be arrested if you accidentally shoot yourself?

2. You must be compensating for something.

3. That gun makes you look fat.

4. Have you tried throwing the bullets instead?

5. You remind me of Elmer Fudd.

6. Is that thing loaded?

7. Do you have a right to bear arms if you're left-handed?

8. Stop! Thief!

9. Does gunpowder make you impotent?

10. Is that a gun in your pocket, or are you just happy to see me?

OFFICE PARTY

1. You give good email.

2. This is just like the party they threw right before the last round of layoffs.

3. I overheard the boss talking—what's a hostile takeover?

4. I've been stealing office supplies.

5. Remember the last holiday party? I don't.

6. You should tell the boss what you really think of him.

7. This is cool because I'm usually drunk at the office anyway.

8. Oh, so *you're* the one who's not getting promoted.

9. Does our health insurance cover medicinal marijuana?

10. Underneath my clothes, I'm wearing nothing but sticky notes.

I SECOND THAT EMOJI

Now that common discourse has moved almost exclusively back to written expression, it stands to reason the quality of our collective pen counts more than ever. But it turns out it's more important to express emotion than use correct syntax. Case in point: a study conducted by New York's Binghamton University showed that texts ending with a period were perceived as less sincere. Deliberately misspelled words, emojis, and yes, even the dreaded exclamation point express the kind of emotional cues that are lacking in digital text-based conversation that constitutes most of our modern communication. So unless you want to look like a huge jerk, do *not* use proper punctuation when you text…period.

WHAT NOT TO SAY IN AN
ONLINE DATING PROFILE

1 My divorce is almost final.

2 Seeking someone with low standards.

3 Nice guys don't always finish last. I finish first.

4 Do you like puppets as much as I do?

5 I enjoy the soothing sounds of the bowling alley.

6 Turn-ons: Chicken gravy.

7 I'm not afraid to cry and I do so after sex. Sometimes during.

8 My ex called me clingy, but I like to think of myself as attentive.

9 Occupation: Youth pastor.

10 My mom says I'm quite a catch.

1 You have insurance, right?

2 How do you spell *emancipation?*

3 Now I know why Mom/Dad hates you.

4 I was thinking about taking a year or two off.

5 It must be nice to get the senior citizen's discount at the movies.

6 You might want to throw that sock out.

7 What was it like back in the old days?

8 You were so good looking when you were young.

9 Do you need to take a nap?

10 Just curious…what are you thinking, inheritance-wise?

THEN THEY CAME FOR JUSTIN BIEBER...

Anne Frank and Justin Bieber seemingly have little in common. Yet both have touched millions of preteens to their emotional cores: one with poignant writings under totalitarian duress, and the other with shrill anthems to adolescent love. And on a Friday in 2013, their legacies were merged when the waifish Canadian troubadour visited Miss Frank's last residence in Amsterdam and wrote in the guestbook: "Truly inspiring to be able to come here. Anne was a great girl. Hopefully she would have been a belieber." The Anne Frank Museum posted his sentiments on their Facebook page, prompting requisite social media outrage. A word to the wise who visit the museum and feel the need to sign its ledger—try not to make everything about *you*.

WHAT NOT TO SAY ON A

PLANE

1. Can I use your under-seat space?

2. I may need to borrow your vomit bag.

3. Nothing calms me down like talking…and talking…

4. There's a pretty good chance migrating birds will be in our flight path.

5. Does that look like a crack in the wing to you?

6. I get nervous on planes, so I apologize now for my inevitable alcohol blackout.

7. Do you think they fixed that problem with the engine?

8. Want some of my anchovy-and-Limburger sandwich?

9. I'm much more comfortable with the armrest up.

10. Can I sleep on your shoulder?

WHAT NOT TO SAY AT A
POOL PARTY

1 I've had some digestive issues lately,
so I'm hoping I feel okay to swim.

2 We prefer to swim in the buff.

3 Will you watch the kids while I go make
a quick phone call?

4 Does the water smell funny to you?

5 Who needs a pool to be warm? It's summer!

6 Don't swim too close to the drain—
it has powerful suction.

7 No one can tell if you pee in the pool.

8 I heard someone drowned in this pool.

9 Some things are better left to the imagination.

10 CANNONBALL!

WHAT NOT TO SAY
TO ANYBODY, EVER

If you
want *my*
opinion...

1 Are you sure it's not twins?

2 You know, vaccinations are evil.

3 You will be breastfeeding, won't you?

4 Pregnancy boobs are the best.

5 You are giving birth naturally, right?

6 Pain medication during childbirth is so dangerous to your baby.

7 You're really thinking of naming the baby *that?*

8 Hopefully you'll get back to fighting weight soon.

9 Do you really think you should eat that?

10 Do you really think you should drink that?

WHAT NOT TO SAY TO THE

RECENTLY DUMPED

1. I saw that coming a mile away.

2. You should never have been a couple in the first place.

3. You guys had no chemistry.

4. I never knew what you saw in her.

5. Finally!

6. You'll make a better choice next time.

7. He can do better.

8. Maybe now you'll have more time for me.

9. Can I hit on her now that she's single?

10. Getting dumped is a great diet.

GESTURE WISELY

As the world gets smaller, hand gestures are becoming more universally understood—but don't count on it. Make sure you aren't innocently gesturing in error. You may think that complimentary thumbs-up is saying "yes, I like it!" but in Iran, Iraq, or Sardinia it will be read as "screw you!" In 1992, the first President Bush flashed the peace "V" to Australian bystanders with his palm inwards. Seems his advance team forgot to tell him it means "up yours" down under, and in England too. The "OK" sign made by circling your finger and thumb? Don't try that in Turkey, Brazil, Venezuela, or France. It might mean "zero" or "worthless" (France) but elsewhere it's really vulgar slang. Really. Vulgar.

1 Are you sure we're from the same gene pool?

2 You're my third favorite.

3 Why aren't you married yet?

4 Do you think our family is racist?

5 Who are you again? I'm really bad with names.

6 You don't look like you're related to us.

7 You're the black sheep.

8 Is what the rest of the family says about you really true?

9 You certainly got the family hairline.

10 In some cultures, we could marry.

WHAT NOT TO SAY IN A
RESTAURANT

1. What do you have that's gluten-free and sustainably farmed?

2. Can you repeat the specials again?

3. This doesn't look like the picture.

4. Do you charge extra for the hair?

5. I'm a Yelper.

6. Now I remember why we never come here.

7. Here's a tip: Fire your chef.

8. I think I'm allergic to that.

9. Nothing for me, I'm trying to eat healthier.

10. Well, *that* was underwhelming.

The ruling consensus seems to be that men channel their insecurities into automotive choices, the odd Prius notwithstanding. That being said, one might assume that marketing one of the earliest American subcompacts would be a politic task to say the least. The balance between man and machine is a delicate one indeed, and the people whose job it was to advertise products should have done their homework or at least stepped more lightly than they did with the Ford Pinto's introduction in Brazil. It seems that in Portuguese, *pinto* means "tiny male genitals." After sales remained stagnant, the name was changed to Corcel.

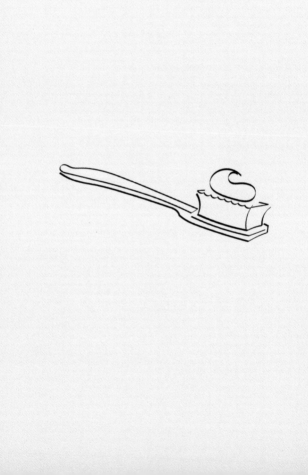

WHAT NOT TO SAY TO A

ROOMMATE

1. My compost heap is really flourishing indoors.

2. It's cool if I pay rent in bitcoin, right?

3. I only flush every other time to conserve water.

4. I used the last of your milk this morning— I can't stand black coffee!

5. Sounded like you two had a *real* good time last night.

6. My boyfriend doesn't live here. He just spends every night here.

7. That scotch was about to expire, so I just finished it.

8. I wouldn't go in there for another 24 hours.

9. I've been feeding the mice so they don't eat our food.

10. I tested your toothbrush.

1 Well, when the president does it, that means it's not illegal.

2 I actually did vote for the $87 billion before I voted against it.

3 This is one of the more impactful and emotional town hall meetings I've ever had. Maybe it's because it's a women's town hall.

4 Life is indeed precious, and I believe the death penalty helps to affirm this fact.

5 You cannot go to a 7-11 or a Dunkin' Donuts unless you have a slight Indian accent. I'm not joking.

<u>6</u> But we have to pass the bill so that you can find out what is in it.

<u>7</u> I think that gay marriage is something that should be between a man and a woman.

<u>8</u> My fear is that the whole island [of Guam] will become so overly populated that it will tip over and capsize.

<u>9</u> It depends upon what the meaning of the word "is" is.

<u>10</u> I remember meeting a mother of a child who was abducted by the North Koreans right here in the Oval Office.

*actual statements from real politicians

WHAT NOT TO SAY
TO ANYBODY, EVER

Everything
happens for
a reason.

WHAT NOT TO SAY DURING

SEX

1. Where should I put this?

2. This isn't my first time.

3. I think I felt it.

4. They're tears of joy.

5. Should you call your doctor?

6. Here goes nothing!

7. Mom?

8. Mexican food was a bad choice.

9. It looked bigger in the picture.

10. What's that smell?

WHAT NOT TO SAY TO A

SHORT PERSON

1   You're not short—you're fun-sized!

2   I bet you can get your clothes in the children's department.

3   I feel so tall around you!

4   Are you proportional?

5   Is that as tall as you are going to get?

6   Do people ever think you are a little person?

7   You're so cute I just want to put you in my pocket!

8   I guess you don't want me to wear heels.

9   My kid is taller than you!

10 You could probably ride that Great Dane.

WHAT NOT TO SAY TO YOUR

SIBLING

1. They didn't take the dog to a farm.

2. At least one of us inherited the family looks.

3. You stole my mommy!

4. I remember when I wanted to be just like you.

5. The sibling rivalry is all in your head.

6. Some of us got over our difficult childhood.

7. You didn't cause *all* of my neuroses.

8. I can't believe we're related.

9. We've gotten used to your eccentricities.

10. I can never take you seriously as an adult.

ARE YOU TALKING TO YOURSELF?

What about what not to say to *yourself*?
"Destructive self-talk" is a relatively common term
used to describe people who blame themselves
for perceived character defects. "*Constructive*
self-talk," on the other hand, is less well known,
yet perhaps far more destructive. While the
former is expressed as negative inner commen-
tary, the latter is a self-affirming cheerleader
who validates even the most misguided choices.
For instance, when you decide a good strategy
during a job interview is to hit on your interviewer,
it may be time to reassess life choices, rather
than reassuring yourself that "perhaps it was
never meant to be and that everything happens
for a reason."

YES, VIRGINIA, JOE BIDEN ACTUALLY SAID THAT

It's often said, "If you don't have anything nice to say, don't say anything at all." That aphorism could be updated for modern times as "If you are Joe Biden, don't say anything at all." In one of his more memorable moments, and an object lesson in how to sound both condescending *and* racist, Biden, when asked his opinion on then Democratic primary opponent Barack Obama, said, "I mean, you got the first mainstream African-American who is articulate and bright and clean and a nice-looking guy. I mean, that's a storybook, man." Biden's remarks, of course, drew rebuke from the press and many members of the African-American community, who rightly took umbrage with the Delaware senator's awkward and politically incorrect phrasing.

WHAT NOT TO SAY TO A

SICK PERSON

<u>1</u> Half of all hospital deaths are attributed to infections contracted while *in* the hospital.

<u>2</u> Fresh air and a brisk walk will cure most anything.

<u>3</u> But you don't look sick.

<u>4</u> Wow, you really look sick.

<u>5</u> I don't think insurance covers that.

<u>6</u> Illness is just a manifestation of some deeper psychological problem.

<u>7</u> Have you heard of Munchausen syndrome?

<u>8</u> If you lost some weight, you'd feel better.

<u>9</u> My cousin died of that.

<u>10</u> Apparently, just when you think you're cured, that condition comes back.

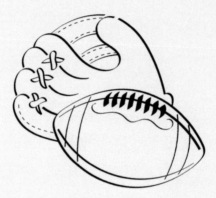

WHAT NOT TO SAY AT A

SPORTING EVENT

1. Who's playing?

2. Do you usually sit this far away?

3. I pee a lot.

4. I hope my agoraphobia doesn't get too intense today.

5. Do we have to stay until the end?

6. Wake me up when it's over.

7. I brought my glove in case someone hits a touchdown.

8. I didn't peg you as the active type.

9. You know this is all fixed, right?

10. The only sport I watch is pro wrestling.

1. You call this artisanal?

2. Do you prosecute shoplifters?

3. It's *how* much?

4. It would look good—with Spanx.

5. Let's eat the free samples instead of going out for lunch.

6. It must be sad selling dead animals.

7. I think I heard something rip.

8. Do I need underwear to try this on?

9. I'm surprised you can make a living selling this.

10. I'd like to return this. I bought it two years ago and have no receipt.

WHAT NOT TO SAY
TO ANYBODY, EVER

I told you so!

1 What happens down here during an earthquake?

2 You look like you need a hug.

3 I think I saw a body on the track.

4 You sat on my invisible friend.

5 Stop the train!

6 Do I smell okay?

7 Wheeeeeee!

8 Just let me squeeze in here.

9 Stop touching me!

10 Can I have a bite?

WHAT NOT TO SAY TO A

TALL PERSON

1. How's the weather up there?

2. You make me feel so short!

3. Guess you can feel the rain before anyone else.

4. You must've played basketball in school.

5. Where do you buy your clothes?

6. What size shoe do you wear?

7. Your parents must be tall.

8. I'll bet you never wear heels.

9. You must have a hard time finding dates.

10. Exactly how tall *are* you?

WHAT NOT TO SAY TO A

TEACHER

1. I wish *I* could leave work at three o'clock every day.

2. Will this be on the exam?

3. I paid a lot for that essay.

4. No one needs to know this crap.

5. How much do you make at this job?

6. At least you're not teaching gym.

7. I had a hot dream about you.

8. I'll just Google it.

9. Must be nice to have summers off.

10. Can I call you Mommy?

WHAT NOT TO SAY ON

VACATION

1. I'm bored.

2. We're tourists!

3. I only speak English.

4. I wish your parents were here.

5. When do we leave again?

6. *I* don't have your passport.

7. I can't stop thinking about work.

8. I might have left the garage door open.

9. We're not interested in the upgrade.

10. Those time-shares sound really interesting.

LOST IN TRANSLATION

Salsa outsells ketchup as one of America's favorite condiments. And as many expatriates living abroad reach for domestic comforts in a strange country, it makes sense that the homesick American might ask for a side of salsa with his Korean pancake. What he might not know is that depending on where he is, he may have just requested a cup of diarrhea instead of the spicy taco sauce. In Korean, the word *salsa* phonetically translates to "diarrhea." So if you are a fan of the Mexican dip, or the Caribbean dance, you might not want to be as vocal about it in Seoul as you would be in Seattle. People might look at you funny when you talk about how sexy "salsa" is.

WHAT NOT TO SAY AT A

WEDDING

<u>1</u> This is the same DJ from the bride's last wedding.

<u>2</u> Statistically, this marriage will probably end in divorce.

<u>3</u> Is there an open bar?

<u>4</u> She's not allowed to wear white.

<u>5</u> Will there be favors?

<u>6</u> They're probably getting married for their taxes.

<u>7</u> Wow, the bride doesn't look pregnant at all.

<u>8</u> I'm here to offer my services. I'm a marriage counselor.

<u>9</u> Who knew cousins could find love like this?

<u>10</u> I hope they play "Electric Slide."

1 You're starting to remind me of your mother.

2 They don't make you look *that* fat.

3 Sure, I was looking at her, but I was thinking about you.

4 Why don't you get my mother's recipe for that?

5 It was only sex—it didn't mean anything.

6 Are you having your period?

7 I wanted to get you something practical.

8 What did you *do* all day?

9 Don't you already have enough shoes?

10 Your sister is looking *good*!

WHAT NOT TO SAY TO ANY

WOMAN

1. You look great for your age.

2. You're a big one, aren't you?

3. You have such a pretty face.

4. What's your natural hair color?

5. When's the baby due?

6. You look so nice when you smile/wear lipstick/ brush your hair.

7. You take everything so personally!

8. You've got quite the appetite for a woman.

9. You're too sensitive.

10. Women!

LIFE MEANS OFTEN HAVING TO SAY YOU'RE SORRY

Should you not heed the advice given in this book and find yourself having delivered one of these lines that has caused offense, consider the simple apology. As Miss Manners says, "The apology is a wonderful thing, indispensable for soothing ruffled if not raging feelings in a volatile society." But, she continues, avoid what she refers to as the "fingers-crossed-behind-the-back" apology, which places blame back on the injured party: "'I'm sorry you feel that way,' or even worse, 'I can understand that you have a problem with that.'" Instead, she suggests a real apology: "I did it. I don't know what I was thinking. I must have been out of my mind. I feel terrible. I promise it will never happen again." Or you could always go with, "I'm sorry."

Created, published, and distributed by Knock Knock
1635 Electric Ave.
Venice, CA 90291
knockknockstuff.com
Knock Knock is a registered trademark of Knock Knock LLC

Illustrations by Michael DeJong

This book is meant solely for entertainment purposes. In no event
will Knock Knock be liable to any reader for any harm, injury, or
damages, including direct, indirect, incidental, special, consequential,
or punitive arising out of or in connection with the use of the
information contained in this book. So there.

ISBN: 978-160106916-0
UPC: 825703-50230-5

10 9 8 7 6 5 4